The College is not intended to fit women for a particular sphere or profession, but to perfect her intellect by the best methods which philosophy and experience suggest, so that she may be better qualified to enjoy and to do well her work in life, whatever that work may be . . . It is a Women's College, aiming not only to give the broadest and highest intellectual culture, but also to preserve and perfect every characteristic of complete womanhood.

President Seelye, in an early circular of Smith College

SMITH COLLEGE

PHOTOGRAPHED BY
TOM SOBOLIK

BLACK STAR

HARMONY HOUSE
PUBLISHERS-LOUISVILLE

Executive Editors: William Butler and William Strode
Library of Congress Catalog Number: 90-81400
Hardcover International Standard Book Number 0-916509-73-7
Printed by D.W. Friesen & Sons Ltd., Manitoba, Canada
First Edition printed Fall, 1990 by Harmony House Publishers,
P.O. Box 90, Prospect, Kentucky 40059 (502) 228-2010 / 228-4446
Copyright © 1990 by Harmony House Publishers
Photographs copyright © 1990 by Tom Sobolik

John M. Greene Hall

INTRODUCTION

A photographic essay of Smith College catalogues memories for us at the same time it envelopes us in the current life of the College. In this collection I find myself happily suspended between two worlds: the one I knew as a student and the one I know today. This balance illustrates an important truth about Smith College: those who have known it as students are forever part of its fabric.

What is it that gives this sense of belonging to all who have known the vitality of Smith? As a freshman, I heard a tiny and vibrant Elizabeth Cutter Morrow, Chairman of the Board of Trustees and then acting President of the College, quote Ada Comstock from the stage of John M. Greene. Miss Comstock had referred to the vast alumnae body (think how much vaster it is today!) as a river forever being fed and forever feeding a strong ongoing stream of women into a waiting world. It struck me even then that if I stood on the bank and watched I could feel myself part of this historic moving stream.

I believe that if each member of the Smith community were asked to list the College's most important strengths, there would be an unusual accord, a strong and common thread clearly discernible through the remarkable variety of our Smith experiences.

Leading the selection would, of course, be the academic experience. Smith College has had every reason to be proud through the years of the quality of its faculty, a group of scholars committed to exciting teaching. Students and faculty share challenges which create an appetite for learning that begins in the classroom and ultimately becomes a lifelong passion. To conquer the intricacies of German sentence structure, to make a Beethoven sonata your own, to grasp the implications of what's going on in Eastern Europe or fathom the federal budget deficit — students today face the same rich choices that students of yesterday knew. There has never been time enough to taste them all.

Another piece of common ground, I believe, would be respect and admiration for the values held important by the College. Early on, Sophia Smith spelled out the ethical truths she believed intrinsic to the institution she was about to establish. In the 109 years since that time, those values have stood fast. What has made Smith College a great institution has been the College's ability to translate those important standards for human behavior into action for more than a century. Respect for the individual and concern for the human condition underlie the directives that Sophia Smith laid out for the College, and these guidelines still help define our actions.

And where on your list of what you value most about Smith College would you put your friends? The downright pleasure of companions, old and young, that you treasured in college multiplies a thousandfold over the years. I heard a prospective student ask recently about the pressure of competition at Smith. The senior who put her mind to rest described Smith as a community of scholars where each student sets her own goals and competes with herself. At the same time, she takes pleasure and pride in the accomplishments of her friends and cohorts. No wonder that Smith College is a place where friends are precious and mutual respect flourishes. The bonds woven by shared pleasures, shared hardships, shared hours together build friendships that long outlast college years. A first encounter with the joyful shrieks of reunion make that very clear.

The unique qualities provided by a college for women would be another important entry on the list. Early generations came, unselfconscious about the reasons and unburdened by the thoughtful decision of today's students to "choose a women's college." But over the years all generations have sensed before leaving Smith the particular rewards of teaching and learning in an institution designed to serve women. It is a satisfying choice to set one's goals for study, for leadership or even for an avocation in a place that offers a promise especially directed to women.

Sophia Smith Bedroom, Alumnae House

Finally the sheer physical beauty of the Smith College campus enchants those who know its bounty. Undergraduates hardly grasp that they are living and working in an arboretum. The more we know it as the years go by, the more we recognize and hold for our own its unlimited treasures.

The finely traced branches of the white Judas trees against the dark walls of Burton may weave a special magic for you. If I were to choose one tree that spells Smith's strength and beauty for me, it would be the handsome Katsura displaying its graceful symmetry for all to admire behind Wright Hall. We recapture many other corners of the campus in memory's eye: an arched bridge and a waterfall, the Quad reflecting the first warm sun of spring, a hillside of daffodils. All this silent beauty has given its lasting touch to our lives almost without our knowing it.

Other memories, too, are stirred by these photographs: ice skaters on Paradise Pond, English muffins and strawberry jam for tea, the dry acrid smell of too much heat in Stoddard Hall on a winter's day. What is it that makes you smile with sweet remembrance? This beautiful and evocative book will, I guarantee, quicken your memory and lift your spirits. I believe it will reinforce for Smith alumnae the pleasure and the power of their Smith experience. For those who know Smith only second-hand, it interprets that experience in an admirable way.

Euphemia Hare Steffey '44
Former Chairman of the Board of Trustees

1870 Sophia Smith's will provides $300,000 for an institution for the higher education of women, its facilities to equal those in colleges for young men.

1871 The town of Northampton, as permitted in the will, gives $25,000 to have the College located in Northampton, instead of in Hatfield; the College is incorporated; the trustees adopt a seal (the Woman of the Apocalypse, after a painting by Murillo), and a motto ("To virtue, knowledge" from II Peter 1:5).

1875 Professor L. Clark Seelye of Amherst College is appointed first president; the College opens with 14 students and three buildings (Dewey House, the President's House and College Hall).

1881 The Alumnae Association is formed by the classes of '80 and '81, the Class of '79 joining later — 47 alumnae in all.

1883 The first women's basketball game is played at Smith.

1887 The first two Smith Clubs organized in Boston and Chicago.

1900 The Quarter Centennial of the opening of the College is celebrated (1,109 students in college; 1,900 have been graduated).

1909 The *Smith Alumnae Quarterly* begins publication; the library is opened (in June 1947 named William Allan Neilson Library).

1910 John M. Greene Hall is first used, at the Baccalaureate Service.

1915 The Sophia Smith homestead in Hatfield is bought by the Alumnae Association (restored and furnished in 1916 by the Class of 1896; deeded to the College in 1946 to hold in perpetuity).

1916 Caps and gowns are worn by the seniors for the first time.

1917 The Smith College Relief Unit is organized by the Alumnae Association; sails for France in August (World War I).

1918 The Smith Training School for Psychiatric Work is established (later called The Smith College School for Social Work).

1919 The president's house on Paradise Road is built.

1921 The great Quadrangle is begun with Ellen Emerson, Jordan and Cushing houses built (completed 1922).

1922 Interdepartmental majors are instituted.

1924 The Grecourt Gates, the memorial to the Smith College Relief Unit, are dedicated.

1925 Juniors study in France, the first group of juniors abroad; the 50th anniversary of the opening of the College is celebrated (2,023 students in college; 10,365 have been graduated).

1933 All students are housed on campus (except for local students living in their own homes).

1938 The Alumnae House is dedicated and deeded to the College.

1942 The Naval Training School for Waves Officers is established at Smith, the Alumnae House serving as staff headquarters until January 1945.

1955 Helen Hills Hills Chapel is completed.

1958 Four valley colleges propose fifth experimental college (opened in 1965 and named Hampshire College).

1964 Male graduate students are admitted.

1970 All curriculum distribution requirements are eliminated; the Committee on Governance recommends increased participation by students in the formulation of educational policy; trustees approve election of the head of student government to the Board of trustees for a two-year term following her graduation.

1971 Parietal rules regarding male visitors in houses are eliminated; men are now allowed in student rooms according to regulations established by each house.

1972 The decision to remain a college predominantly for women is approved by the Board of Trustees.

1974 The College begins a year-long celebration of its Centennial at September convocation.

1975 The Ada Comstock Scholars Program — for older women students — is approved by faculty; inauguration of Jill Ker Conway as seventh president, first woman president.

1976 Class of 1980 enters, the largest freshman class in Smith College history (781 students).

1984 Smith College faculty approves academic minors.

1985 Senda Berenson, director of physical training at Smith from 1892-1911, is elected to the Basketball Hall of Fame; inauguration of Mary Maples Dunn as eighth president.

1986 A racial slur painted on the steps of Lilly Hall prompts a college-wide effort to enhance equality in all phases of campus life; the Board of Trustees votes to divest by October 1988 all holdings in companies that do business in South Africa.

1987 The largest capital fund drive by any women's college begins. The Campaign for Smith seeks $125 million; by 1989 has raised more than $163 million.

1988 *The Smith Design for Institutional Diversity* is endorsed by the Board of Trustees; The Design outlines goals for increasing diversity in the campus community and college curriculum.

I think the first quality of the college that I especially like is the feeling it gives to each of us, whether teacher or student, of belonging to a community, not of "noble souls made perfect" by scholarship and enlightenment, but simply a community of people, middle-aged and young, interested in discovering the inseparable relation-ship between learning and life, and at the same time thoroughly enjoying each part of that combination.

Professor Mary Ellen Chase, from "Smith College — A Definition" in the *Smith Alumnae Quarterly*

Lamont Bridge

28

Paradise Pond Dam

Overleaf: College Hall

The Quadrangle

Preceding page: center campus from Seelye Hall

Lanning Fountain

Botanic Gardens

Annual spring bulb show in Lyman Plant House

President's House

Opening Convocation

Reading in the Browsing Room

Neilson Library

*Overleaf: Josten Library in the Mendenhall
Center for the Performing Arts*

48   *College Archives in the Alumnae Gym*

Although the curriculum here in many ways is very similar in its content and its structure to other institutions of equal educational quality, in other ways it is not. It is different because it takes women's experience into account, makes your direct knowledge of youselves the starting point for critical thinking and urges you to build models of explanation, in any field, which take their roots from that experience and take it seriously.

President Jill Ker Conway

Rare Book Room in Neilson Library

Outdoors the campus is so charming that one either girds oneself to resist it or succumbs to what might be terminal bucolitis: in fact a number of people have —alumnae make up a quarter of Smith's administrative staff. Within the Quadrangle or overlooking Paradise Pond, it is so beautiful that it seems a campus a Hollywood set designer might have created.

Elizabeth Stone, in *Ms*, May 1979, "What Can An All-Women's College Do For Women?'

Hallie Flanagan Studio Theatre

Smithereens performance

Museum of Art

In women's institutions women experience autonomy and power; there are no choices they cannot make freely and without those subtle social obstacles which still suggest to women that there are things we shouldn't do.

President Mary Maples Dunn, in her inaugural address, 1985

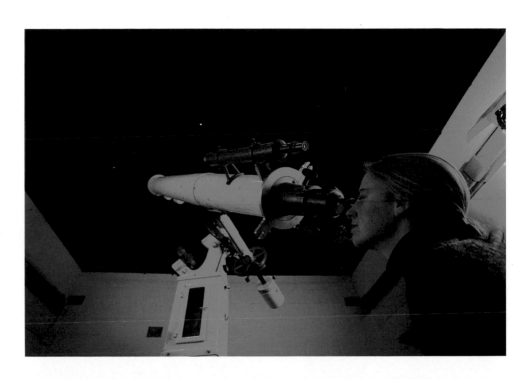

I like the atmosphere at Smith. It was one in which we had freedom academically to do what we wanted within the very liberal restrictions. Of course, had I been more mature I would have done possibly other things. But I certainly got a varied and good foundation. I had science and language, government, literature, all kinds of things and I was certainly in contact with some marvelous minds. I was always happy there.

Julia Child '34, in *College: A Smith Mosaic*

Studying Art History

Alumnae Association Library

Debate team

College should be a four years of not only learning and exposing yourself to lots of different thoughts and ideas and courses but also four years of finding yourself as a person and setting the mold. Lots of extra things come into that — there's nothing wrong with going out and cheering at a football game and eating hot dogs and going on picnics and having a good time, it's all part of it. And it's the only time in your life that you can do it.

Nancy Davis Reagan '43, in *College: A Smith Mosaic*

Rally Day Convocation

Overleaf: Hopkins House

65

Spring Weekend party

Indoor Track and Tennis Facility

The game that was most adapted to women and most popular was basketball from the very beginning. Senda Berenson, the director of physical training in 1892, went down to Spring-field where James Naismith had invented it, saw it, and decided it was a good game for girls. She brought it up and she and the girls drew up those first rules for girls.

Dorothy Sears Ainsworth '16

It was a very exciting campus to live on. There was an air of anticipation about it. People wanting to do things. I can remember waking up each morning feeling terribly excited about getting started with the day. I hadn't ever had that big a sense of exhilaration before I went to Smith.

Mary Eckman Switkay '49, in *College: A Smith Mosaic*

Helen Hills Hills Chapel

The chief business of the College . . . is mental culture. It is neither a sanitarium nor a sanctuary. Its distinctive object is mental perfection. That perfection can never be secured, if the College pays no attention to physical and spiritual soundness . . . For its own integrity, for the proper accomphishment of its end, the College must care for the spiritual condition of its students.

President Seelye

Senior Ball

Ivy Day

And then comes the end toward which the four happy crowded years have been tending; and wandering over the campus in the last June twilights the Senior is not ashamed of the drops that fill her eyes, or the choking that makes it impossible for her to join in the song to Alma Mater who "Gave us dreams unnumbered, and life we had not known," but strong in love and rich in desire to do, she goes forth to answer the call of the larger world and so to answer it as to bring honor to the College that helped her find herself.

President Seelye, in *The Early History of Smith College, 1871-1910*

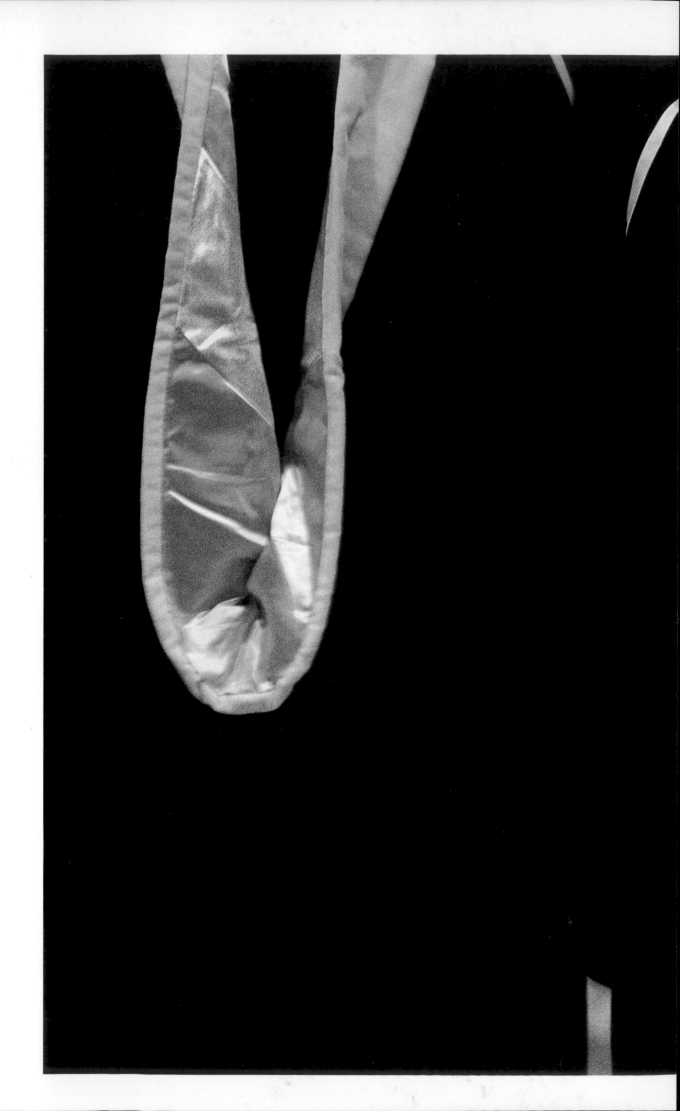

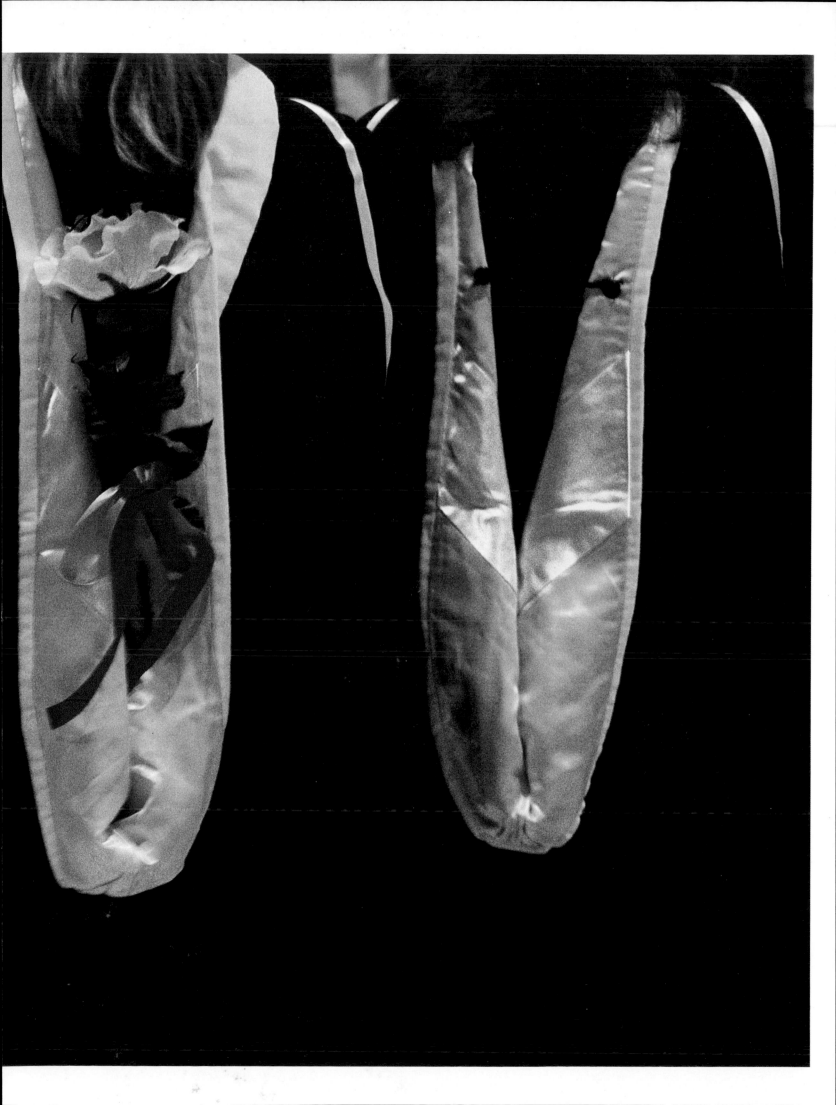

A BACKWARD GLANCE

Photographs from the Smith College Photographic Archives

A campus panorama, ca. 1920. Left to right are Neilson Lab, Hatfield, John M. Greene, Wallace House, St. John's Church, Old Hillyer Art Gallery and Seelye Hall.

John M. Greene, Sophia Smith's pastor, who persuaded her to found a college with her estate.

This building, shown here in 1910, has served the College as the President's house, Gateway House, the Infirmary and the Dean's House.

The founder, Sophia Smith.

The "Main" Building, 1895.

L. Clark Seelye, President of Smith College, 1873-1910, is shown here in the last year of his presidency.

President William Allen Neilson in June, 1923.

Alumnae Gym (left) and Lawrence House (under construction) in the winter of 1891.

The William Allen Neilson Library, 1938.

Wallace House and Dewey House, 1904.

Hubbard, Washburn, Hatfield and Dewey, around 1887.

Students walk from Neilson
Library in 1915.

Haven House, 1932.

The Chapel in Social Hall (College Hall) in 1904.

Horticulture class in the
Lyman Plant House, 1900.

The Lyman Plant House was
also the scene of this Science
Lab in 1904.

Seelye Hall Library, circa 1900.

The Sitting Room
of Dewey Hall,
circa 1890.

The College's first Library was on the
second floor of College Hall, shown
here in the 1890s.

Registrar Mary Eastman reads aloud to students as they knit in Haven House, 1911.

The Browsing Room of the Neilson Library, 1943.

The Hubbard House tennis courts, circa 1890.

Inter-class basketball game in College Hall, 1901.

Outdoor basketball on Allen Field, 1912.

Ice hockey on the pond, winter, 1931.

Crew, early 1940s.

A softball game, 1920s.

On the archery range, 1920s.

Faculty vs. students in a softball game, 1954.

In 1901 field hockey was introduced at Smith. In the background, left to right, are the Observatory, Wallace House, Hatfield and the Old Gym.

The field hockey team, 1929.

The hockey team in action, 1950.

The dedication of the Grécourt Gates, October 18, 1924. Left to right are: President Neilson, Harriet (Boyd) Hawes, Class of 1892, who organized the Smith College Relief Unit in France for which the Gates are a commemoration, M. Gaston Liebert, former French Consul in New York and Ada L. Comstock, Class of 1897, president of Radcliffe College.